Build It From A to Z

Trish Holland

TeachingStrategies™ • Washington D.C.

For Teaching Strategies, Inc.
Publisher: Larry Bram
Editorial Director: Hilary Parrish Nelson
VP Curriculum and Assessment: Cate Heroman
Product Manager: Kai-leé Berke
Book Development Team: Sherrie Rudick and Jan Greenberg
Project Manager: Jo A. Wilson

For Q2AMedia
Editorial Director: Bonnie Dobkin
Editor and Curriculum Adviser: Suzanne Barchers
Program Manager: Gayatri Singh
Creative Director: Simmi Sikka
Project Manager: Santosh Vasudevan
Designers: Ritu Chopra & Shruti Aggarwal
Picture Researcher: Anita Gill

Picture Credits
t-top b-bottom c-center l-left r-right

Cover: Mike Clarke/Istockphoto.

Back Cover: Shutterstock.

Title page: Aba Ssaka/Shutterstock.

Insides: Zsolt Nyulaszi/Shutterstock: 3, Fotog/Photolibrary: 4, Karlien du Plessis/Shutterstock: 5, Amy Myers/Dreamstime: 6, Masterfile: 7, Susan Law Cain/Dreamstime: 8, Mark Atkins/ Dreamstime: 9, Peter Close/Shutterstock: 10, Wave RF/ Photolibrary: 11, Corbis Superstock: 12, prism68/Shutterstock: 13, Andrew Rich /Istockphoto: 14, Constantin Opris/Dreamstime: 15, Claudio Bertoloni/Shutterstock: 16, Marcel Pelletier/ Istockphoto: 17, Masterfile: 18, Thinkstock/Jupiter Images: 19, Nancy Everest/Istockphoto: 20, Christina Richards/Shutterstock: 21, Aba Ssaka/Shutterstock: 22, Matt Jacques/Dreamstime: 23, Maxstockphoto/Shutterstock: 24.

Teaching Strategies, Inc.
P.O. Box 42243
Washington, DC 20015
www.TeachingStrategies.com

ISBN: 978-1-60617-136-3

Library of Congress Cataloging-in-Publication Data
Holland, Trish.
  Build it from A to Z / Trish Holland.
    p. cm.
  ISBN 978-1-60617-136-3
  1. Building--Juvenile literature. 2. Alphabet books--Juvenile literature. I. Title.
  TH149.H645 2010
  690--dc22
                              2009036779

CPSIA tracking label information:
RR Donnelley, Shenzhen, China
Date of Production: July 2015
Cohort: Batch 4

Printed and bound in China

 6 7 8 9 10   15
_____   _____

   Printing   Year Printed

Aa

is for **a**rchitect.

An architect designs a building. How tall?
How wide? Will it be brick or concrete or wood?
Where will the windows and doors go? She draws
plans called "blueprints." All the answers are there.

Bb

is for **b**ulldozer.

A bulldozer bustles back and forth to clear
space for a new building. The bulldozer pushes
dirt and debris away. Now builders can begin.

Cc

is for **c**oncrete.

A concrete mixer churns as it combines cement,
sand, tiny rocks, and water to make concrete.
When the concrete is ready, it slides down
the chute. The concrete will dry as hard as stone.

Dd

is for **d**ump truck.

A dump truck delivers dirt, sand,
or gravel for construction. The driver
tilts the back, and the load pours down.

Ee

is for **e**ngineer.

An engineer examines the plans for elevators,
escalators, and electric lights. He makes sure
everything in the building will work once it's built.

F f

is for **f**orklift.

A forklift ferries weighty materials for construction.
Its back end is heavy so it doesn't tip over in front
when it picks up a heavy load.

Gg

is for **g**rader.

A grader scrapes at the dirt. It goes over and over the area until the ground is level. The grader grumbles and growls loudly as it works.

Hh
is for **h**ard **h**at.

Ii
is for **i**nspector.

A building inspector wears a hard hat. She knows all the city's construction rules. She inspects a building inside and out to see that the rules are followed. The hard hat helps keep her safe.

Jj

is for **j**igsaw.

A carpenter uses a jigsaw to cut shapes into wood.
The saw has jagged teeth that jiggle up and down.
Sawdust flies as the carpenter cuts out shapes.

Kk

is for **k**eep out.

A "keep out" sign tells people to stay away.
Holes, falling objects, and big moving machines
are just some of the dangers at a construction site.

Ll

is for **l**adder.

Mm

is for **m**ason.

A mason climbs a long ladder to lay bricks
for a tall wall. It takes many thousands
of bricks to make a whole building.

Nn

is for **n**ails.

Construction workers hammer nails all
over a new building. Large nails hold the
building's frame together. Smaller nails are
used for jobs like window frames and shelves.

Oo
is for **o**veralls.

Pp
is for **p**ainter.

A painter wears overalls to protect his
other clothes from paint spatters. Often
he is covered in paint by the end of the day.

Qq

is for **q**uarry.

Stone comes from a quarry. Granite, marble, and limestone can be used in buildings. Workers take blocks or long slabs from the earth with big machines. A quarry is a noisy place.

Rr

is for **r**oof.

Every house has a roof on top. Some roofs are covered with shingles. Others are made of metal, tile, fiberglass, or even rubber!

S s

is for **s**aw

T t

is for **t**oolbox.

A construction worker takes his toolbox to work
every day. It holds saws, screwdrivers, screws,
soldering irons, scissors, and much more—
everything he needs to do a terrific job.

18

Uu

is for **u**tility pole.

A utility pole holds up phone and electric lines outside. The lines run from the pole to the building. Sometimes utility lines run underground instead.

Vv

is for **v**arnish.

Painters may cover wood with varnish to make
it very shiny. The varnish also protects the wood.
While varnish is wet, it can smell like pine trees
because it is sometimes made with pine tree resin.

W w

is for **w**heelbarrow.

A worker whisks a wheelbarrow around
a construction site. He takes dirt, concrete,
gravel, or sand wherever it is needed.

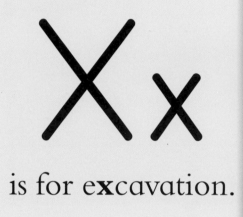

Xx

is for e**x**cavation.

Digging the hole for a building's foundation and basement is called excavation. An excavator scoops up the dirt and drops it into a dump truck.

22

Y y is for **y**ellow.

Z z is for **z**one.

A construction zone sign is often yellow. The yellow color tells people nearby to be careful. Trucks, machines, and workers are always on the go. A construction zone is a busy place.

Can you think of other
words about building?
Build them—from A to Z!

Aa Bb Cc Dd Ee
Ff Gg Hh Ii Jj Kk
Ll Mm Nn Oo Pp
Qq Rr Ss Tt Uu
Vv Ww Xx Yy Zz